To:

_____

From:

_____

Date:

_____

© 2004 by Barbour Publishing, Inc.

ISBN 1-59789-099-5

Cover image © Greg Jackson
Designed by Greg Jackson, Thinkpen Design, LLC.

Scripture quotations are taken from the King James Version of the Bible.

Published by Barbour Publishing, Inc., P.O. Box 719, Uhrichsville, Ohio 44683
www.barbourbooks.com

*Our mission is to publish and distribute inspirational products offering
exceptional value and biblical encouragement to the masses.*

Member of the
Evangelical Christian
Publishers Association

Printed in China.
5 4 3 2 1

A Father Is...

BARBOUR
PUBLISHING

RACHEL QUILLIN

Dear Dad,
What a
blessing
you are!

Thank you for investing so much time and being into the lives of your children. It makes all the difference in the world and in the course of eternity to have a godly man rearing and directing godly children. Your spiritual leadership helps sustain your children. The love you have for your children gives them confidence even though they reside in a cruel world. Your friendship assures them that they are worthwhile. Your direction and example provide a blueprint that guides your children to become productive individuals. You truly are a gift from God!

A Father Is. . .

LOVE

Many waters
cannot quench love,
neither can the
floods drown it:
if a man would give
all the substance
of his house
for love,
it would utterly
be contemned.

Song of Solomon 8:7

*To her,
the name
of father was
another name
for love.*

Fanny Fern

And walk in love, as
Christ also hath loved us,
and hath given himself
for us an offering and
a sacrifice to God for a
sweet-smelling savour.

Ephesians 5:2

Love Notes

Children never outgrow the need for love and encouragement, and good dads never outgrow the desire to lavish their children with these blessings. My dad hasn't outgrown it yet. He still tells me regularly that he loves me, and he often gives me a hug to go with his words. These gestures might seem trivial to some, and I suppose that's because so often they are meaningless. For me they carry great weight. I know they are special and backed by complete truth.

A father's love and affection can go a long way in brightening a child's day, and Dad knows that. During my summers off from college, I worked in the shipping department of a large paintbrush company. Generally I had to be there at 7 a.m., but sometimes it was as early as 6 o'clock. Mornings were not the best time of day for me, and I tried to squeeze in as many moments of precious sleep as possible. Dad knew me well enough to realize how much I could use those extra moments, so each morning he would pack my lunch so I wouldn't have to. I really appreciated it and was not ashamed to let my coworkers in on my secret. Sometimes they teased me about being spoiled, but I didn't care. I enjoyed those lunches.

Sometimes Dad would add an extra treat like a Reese's cup or a couple of chocolate Kisses. Those always made me smile, but what I appreciated most were the notes. So often I would find a note on my napkin that said, "I love you. I'm praying for you." Although I enjoyed my job, it could get monotonous at times, and those notes always brought smiles in the middle of long days.

What an encouragement to know that someone who loved me was offering prayers on my behalf and that Someone who loved me even more was answering those prayers. And you know what? It's still true today. Dad still loves and prays for me, and my heavenly Father still loves me and answers those prayers. What better gifts could a child ask for?

*The most important
thing a father can do
for his children is
to love their mother.*

Henry Ward Beecher

A Father Is. . .

A MENTOR

A father, in addition to being a parent, is a provider, a mentor, a teacher, a friend.

Dad always provided for his family. Times were tough some years, but Dad, along with resourcefulness from Mom, made sure we had a home, food, and clothing. We never knew we were poor back then. Dad made things fun. We enjoyed playing with him as youngsters. I always respected my dad as a mentor. He loved me, and I knew it. What a joy to know the love of a parent.

I live next door to my dad, which has been a blessing through the years. Dad still listens to my problems and offers advice. He is a teacher also. He has taught me to many things—especially "guy" things like using tools, hanging drywall, driving a boat, and mowing the lawn. I very much appreciate knowing how to do these things.

Today I consider my dad more than a parent. He is a friend. We talk to each other as friends. As an adult, I value this friendship. Dad can also be ornery and humorous, which are important ingredients in life. He cares deeply for his family—his wife, his children, his grandchildren, and his great-grandchildren. I love and respect my dad for all this and more.

DONNA K. WARNER

Train up a child in the way he
should go: and when he is old,
he will not depart from it.

PROVERBS 22:6

*Small boys become big men
through the influence of big men
who care about small boys.*

ANONYMOUS

Correct thy son,
and he shall
give thee rest; yea,
he shall give delight
unto thy soul.

PROVERBS 29:17

I was always so impressed with how strong my dad was. He grew up a farm kid and finished growing up as a sailor in WWII. From those experiences, he gained the strength in his arms and his hands—and in his mind—to do anything that ever needed to be done. I remember (when I was little) thinking that he could fix anything. . .including me! I knew not to challenge him, because he could take me down. As a teenager, I knew he could take on any guy I might bring home.

As an adult, I've come to appreciate just how much of that "strength" I need in raising my own kids. I've seen Dad's strength in ways he's always available to help out with any of our household projects, how he can watch over all of his grandkids and command the respect he deserves just by the mere strength he possesses in disciplining the kids when they need it. As he grows older, the physical strength has begun to wane (that trick knee keeps acting up), but his mental and emotional strengths have grown. He still takes great care of all of us, especially Mom. How lucky I am to still have both my parents! As long as they're alive, they're still the adults, and I'm still the child. I like that!

EILEEN HACKETT

Dear Heavenly Father,
The men You have placed in the role of
fatherhood have a wonderful privilege
and a great responsibility. Please guide
each one as he strives to mold the thinking
of his children in a way that pleases You.
Help the fathers of today encourage their
sons and daughters to do their best. God,
You know that a man's attitude toward
his children plays a big role in their
perception of themselves. Help our dads to
remember that they are indeed preparing
our future leaders. Help them determine
to guide their children—to teach them to
make wise choices. Help them to be their
children's biggest supporter and to love
them no matter what. Thank You, Lord, for
being the best example any dad could look
to. Amen.

*One father is more
than a hundred
schoolmasters.*

GEORGE HERBERT

And he did that
which was right in
the sight of the LORD.

2 KINGS 15:3

I will behave myself wisely
in a perfect way. O when
wilt thou come unto me?
I will walk within my house
with a perfect heart.

PSALM 101:2

A Father Is. . .

A SPIRITUAL LEADER

And if it seem evil unto you to serve the LORD, choose you this day whom ye will serve; whether the gods which your fathers served that were on the other side of the flood, or the gods of the Amorites, in whose land ye dwell: but as for me and my house, we will serve the LORD.

JOSHUA 24:15

And he said unto them,
Set your hearts unto
all the words which
I testify among you
this day, which ye shall
command your children
to observe to do, all
the words of this law.

DEUTERONOMY 32:46

Noah's Ark

Growing up as a pastor's kid had both advantages and disadvantages, but in my mind the advantages far outweigh their competition. My dad is a godly man; he is also a very intelligent man, especially where the Bible is concerned. He has pastored for more than thirty years and taught classes at a Bible college for part of that time. Always his sermons and lectures are geared toward his audiences. He doesn't try to impress people with his words; he preaches and teaches and prays that God will use his lips to reach the hearts of his listeners.

Dad has always known that it is just as important to reach the hearts of children as it is to reach the hearts of adults. He especially wanted to make sure that while attending to the needs of the church, he didn't lose his own kids spiritually. Because of this, he spent time making the Bible come alive for us. I remember one time in particular. We were having family devotions. He took us into the kitchen, pulled a bench to the sink, and had us climb onto it. He ran water in the sink and put a little plastic boat in the water. Then he told the story of Noah's ark. When it was time for the flood, he made sure he put the little boat under the faucet and turned the water on full force. We had such fun watching the little boat bobbing up and down. It was a simple illustration really, and a very common Bible story as well, but he took the time to make it special for us. That told us two things: We were important to him; and he wanted the Bible to be important to us.

Dad is still a spiritual leader for me today even though I'm grown and have my own family. I often call him with questions about the Bible or ask his advice on spiritual issues. He loves to discuss God's Word, and he pays attention to what it really says instead of trying to make it say what he wants it to say. What a blessing to have a father who wants me to know God's best for me.

The living, the living,
he shall praise thee, as
I do this day: the father
to the children shall
make known thy truth.

Isaiah 38:19

*A good example is
the best sermon.*

Anonymous

Gather me the people
together, and I will make
them hear my words,
that they may learn to
fear me all the days that
they shall live upon the
earth, and that they may
teach their children.

Deuteronomy 4:10

For I know him,
that he will command
his children and his
household after him,
and they shall keep
the way of the LORD, to
do justice and judgment.

GENESIS 18:19

*Dear Lord Jesus,
Thank You for the wonderful
men who bear the name "Father."
Please bless each one, and help
them daily to be the best dads
they can be. Use them each in a
mighty way to be the leaders they
should be. Through their influence,
may this world be changed for You.
Thank You, Jesus. Amen.*

*My father used to play
with my brother and me
in the yard. Mother
would come out and say,
"You're tearing up the grass."
"We're not raising grass,"
Dad would reply.
"We're raising boys."*

HARMON KILLEBREW

A Father Is. . .

A FRIEND

Dear Jesus,
You are our friend who sticks closer than a
brother. At the same time, You are our lov-
ing heavenly Father. Thank You for show-
ing us that it is possible for a man to be
both father and friend. Thank You for dads
who are willing to spend time just having
fun with their children. They've realized
that those times of play can be some of
the best teachable moments they will ever
have access to. They also know that time
spent in play is time spent in love. Dads
who are their children's friends rejoice in
their children's happy moments and give
strength in times of discouragement. Thank
You, Lord, for men who are not afraid to
be both father and friend.
Amen.

*Blessed indeed is
the man who hears
many gentle voices
call him father.*

LYDIA M. CHILD

*'Tis a happy thing
to be the father
unto many sons.*

WILLIAM SHAKESPEARE

A friend loveth
at all times, and
a brother is born
for adversity.

Proverbs 17:17

Tickle Beasts and Tweaky Indians

Dad is still a kid at heart. For some people, being around kids makes them old, but it has just the opposite effect on Dad. He loves kids—especially his kids—and he loves kids' games. While he no longer cannonballs off the diving board to grab one of us in the swimming pool, it is a common sight to see him down on the floor tickling his granddaughter or galloping around with his grandson on his shoulders. Hearing the kids squeal with delight is one of the things in life that makes him the happiest.

It's always been that way. Many of my fondest childhood memories are of Saturday evenings. We never watched a lot of television while I was growing up, but just about every Saturday evening we would watch Mutual of Omaha's *Wild Kingdom*. It was not unusual afterward for all of us kids and Dad to be on the floor reenacting (with much artistic license) the program we had just seen. We especially liked the African shows. We would see a program about lions and their prey. The helpless wildebeest was one of the lion's favorite victims. In our rendition, however, the wildebeest was converted to a lurking predator, the tickle beast (aka Dad), who stalked his own helpless victims (aka us kids), quickly pounced upon them, and tickled them mercilessly until they either surrendered or somehow managed to wriggle free.

We enjoyed many of the other shows and our own dramas afterward. The playtimes were special times with Dad. He always had a way to make any experience fun. I remember when I was quite small, Dad created a Tweaky Indian. This was a character I never saw but will never forget. Whenever we went hiking, he would tell me to watch out for these Tweaky Indians. They weren't dangerous, but they did like to sneak up on those who weren't cautious and "tweak" their ears. I often had my earlobe tweaked by one of these individuals, but by the time I turned around, whoever had done it had mysteriously slipped back into the woods, leaving no trace. I'm still on the lookout for Tweakies today when I find myself on a trail in the woods, and I certainly plan to make sure that my children are aware of these gentle, but sneaky, people.

It's amazing how children pick up on the love that is displayed in simple childhood games. Although we might have been breathless from laughter at being tickled so much, we were always secure in the knowledge that Dad loved us. That knowledge stays with us yet. We don't really enjoy being tickled anymore, but Dad has other fun ways of showing us that he still loves us.

A Father Is. . .

AN EXAMPLE

The just
man walketh
in his integrity:
his children
are blessed
after him.

PROVERBS 20:7

And, ye fathers, provoke
not your children to
wrath: but bring them
up in the nurture and
admonition of the Lord.

Ephesians 6:4

*No one like one's
mother and father
ever lived.*

Robert T. S. Lowell

Ye are the light
of the world.
A city that is
set on a hill
cannot be hid.

Matthew 5:14

*My father didn't
tell me how to live;
he lived, and let me
watch him do it.*

Clarence Budington Kelland

None of you can ever be proud enough of being the child of such a father who has not his equal in this world—so great, so good, so faultless. Try, all of you, to follow in his footsteps and don't be discouraged, for to be really in everything like him none of you, I am sure, will ever be. Try, therefore, to be like him in some points, and you will have acquired a great deal.

VICTORIA, QUEEN OF ENGLAND

A Glimpse of Jesus

I look at you and get a glimpse
Of my Savior, Jesus Christ.
It's not hard for me to love Him,
Seeing He is in your life.

I know you prayed so faithfully
That to Christ my life I'd give.
Now you teach by your example,
And you show me how to live.

Because your love for me is great,
I know God's love is greater still.
And what you've shown me by your life
Helps me want to seek God's will.

I thank my heavenly Father
For the wisdom He has shown
In making you my father here—
A great gift I've surely known.

RACHEL QUILLIN

A father is:
An unfailing provider,
An unyielding but loving
hand of correction,
A beacon through
the storms of life,
A spiritual anchor,
An advocate for
his children,
A teacher,
An architect of
nations' futures.

DAVID M. GREEGOR

I watched a small man with thick calluses on both hands work fifteen and sixteen hours a day. I saw him once literally bleed from the bottoms of his feet, a man who came here uneducated, alone, unable to speak the language, who taught me all I needed to know about faith and hard work by the simple eloquence of his example.

MARIO CUOMO

*My father opens the door
to my heart and soul when
he plays the old hymns on
his guitar and harmonica.
What a blessing he is to me.
He's the one who cares when
it seems no one else does.*

Katherine Greegor

A Father Is. . .

A GIFT
FROM GOD

To be in your child's memories tomorrow, you have to be in their lives today.

UNKNOWN

Dear God,
The blessing You have bestowed
upon this world in our earthly
fathers is truly indescribable. We
cannot begin to express the depths
of our gratitude for the men in our
lives who have held us in our
earliest hours, directed us during
our most vulnerable years, and
loved us throughout our lives.
Thank You, God, for the gift
of fathers. Amen.

If a son shall ask bread of any
of you that is a father, will he
give him a stone? or if he ask a fish,
will he for a fish give him a
serpent? Or if he shall ask an egg,
will he offer him a scorpion? If ye
then, being evil, know how to give
good gifts unto your children:
how much more shall your
heavenly Father give the Holy
Spirit to them that ask him?

Luke 11:11–13

My Father

Every daughter likes to think
That her father is the best,
But there's no doubt for me, Dad,
That you're far above the rest.

When I was a little girl
You took time to play with me.
You'd wrestle, read, or color,
Though so tired you would be.

You knew that play was not enough
To make the greatest dad.
You also shared God's love for me,
And for this I'm very glad.

Your godly life has made you
The best father there could be;
You've followed God's example
Of what a father should be.

I love you, Father, on this day
As well as on the rest.
No dad on earth compares to you.
You simply are the best.

RACHEL QUILLIN

*A father is
always there to
support and
protect you.*

Jessica Wertz

A good man leaveth
an inheritance to his
children's children: and
the wealth of the sinner
is laid up for the just.

Proverbs 13:22

My father is gently strong. [He] has used his strength to spank me when I did wrong, hug me and say, "I love you," and to protect me when my life was out of control. Even as he ages, my love and respect for him grow. Until the day he is laid to rest, my father will always teach me, love me, and protect me with all of his strength.

PATTY BECKER

Fathers, provoke
not your children
to anger, lest they
be discouraged.

COLOSSIANS 3:21

*By profession,
I am a soldier
and take pride
in that fact.
But I am prouder—
infinitely prouder—
to be a father. . . .*

DOUGLAS MACARTHUR

A Father's Prayer

Dear Heavenly Father,
Thank You for being the best example of a
father that I can look to, and thank You for
offering wisdom in Your holy Word that I can
go to for guidance. Please help me to love my
children the way that You love me, and when
discipline is necessary, help me to lovingly
administer what is needed the way that You
do for me. Help me to guide and direct in
a godly way. Help me to have fun with my
children and to provide a secure environment
that will allow my kids to feel confident in
who they are. Please help me to be a spiritual
leader—one who emphasizes the importance
of a close relationship with You. And Father,
constantly remind me of what a blessed man
I am to be a father. In the good times and
the bad, help me to remember that my
children are a wonderful gift from You.
Thank You, Father. Amen.